MW01224488

Dreams Squibbles & Poetry

Brother
to
Sister
with all my love

Jorge K

Oct 14 2010

authorHOUSE®

AuthorHouse™
1663 Liberty Drive
Bloomington, IN 47403
www.authorhouse.com
Phone: 1-800-839-8640

© *2010 Jorge K. All rights reserved.*

No part of this book may be reproduced, stored in a retrieval system, or transmitted by any means without the written permission of the author.

First published by AuthorHouse   6/16/2010

ISBN: 978-1-4520-1951-2 (e)
ISBN: 978-1-4520-1957-4 (sc)

Library of Congress Control Number: 2010906525

Printed in the United States of America
Bloomington, Indiana

This book is printed on acid-free paper.

*Dedicated
to lucid dreamers
with a sense of humor*

Contents

Dreams

May 31 1986

PART 1

The president of the United States, flying in a helicopter near the Atlantic coast of France was pursuing or was being pursued by other helicopters in the vicinity. Though out of sight, I had the impression there were many helicopters in the air. Suddenly the sky illuminated from a giant explosion roughly located over Northern Africa. I knew that it was an atomic bomb. Soon after that, a second explosion occurred over Great Britain.

PART 2

Somewhere in a big North American city people were gathered in the streets gazing at glass buildings, making no attempt to run. There was no place to run. They were looking straight into the radiation, fire.

PART 3

In another location in North America, people were running about frantically trying to get something organized. Some sort of device was lying on the ground in pieces. A woman near by knew its purpose but refused to tell me what it was. I gave her my sincere apology and embraced her. Then pointing at the machine she started to explain how when these upper things were connected to these lower things a certain specific function was performed. Later I had the understanding that this device would be used to tap the sunlight for the human race on Earth.

PART 4

I was in a pick-up truck with two men that I did not know. I made a reference to the bible. I asked if they knew the story of Noah's Ark. They said they did and I remarked that we were living it again, except this time instead of water we would be covered in a very light and dirty substance. I said we are still responsible for gathering or bringing together all species of plant and living creatures in couples. The two men looked at me in disbelief. I felt surprised and disappointed that these two people were unaware of the possibility of salvation. Then I said, "Noah's Ark – take two." They looked at me in surprise. As we drove along the coast, a series of small sail boats were moored all in a row. Each boat could hold five to ten people and each had a single mast. No sails were unfurled.

August 14 1983

My father brought me into a very large chamber. Most of the room was painted gold and black. There were some statues that looked like they belonged to a very ancient period in Egyptian history. Massive columns supported a ceiling painted with many stars. I could see the Milky Way, nebulas and many galaxies. As I continued to gaze I felt as though I was in deep space. My father said that the dense 'light forms' had been taken away and this was all that was left. I felt that my small life was part of a bigger picture. I had the sensation of floating among the stars in a sort of celestial playground; becoming one with them. Then I heard a calling as though to a new and higher level, but felt unprepared and went off into another dream.

August 5 1981

An enormous snake lay beheaded on the ground. We were at the site of a large ancient ruin. We went inside a building and amongst the debris my companion found the head which was almost as big as his own. I picked up the small sword which was used in slaying the giant creature. The blade was about sixteen inches long. It had engravings running up the middle on either side and on the "T" shaped hilt, which was rounded at the bottom.

As we left the building my companion expressed disbelief that such a small sword could be used to slay such a large serpent.

We came to a boy of thirteen or fourteen years of age, and laid artifacts before him. He took the sword and went to the extreme end of a slightly tilted ramp. With a simple cloth around his mid section, he had the appearance of a young mythological Greek god. He had curly golden hair, clear eyes, richly tanned skin and a radiant face. With the sword in hand, he knelt before his father.

My companion and I went into a theatre. The high ceiling slanted towards the back of the large room. There were thousands of people inside. Along the walls were many doors and stairways. The massive ceiling slowly slid back and people were leaving their seats as though the day of liberation had come. They were moving up the stairways and disappearing beyond the doors. It seemed that the ceiling was composed of large slow moving slabs enclosing the extremes of the building and in the unseen distance other slabs were being triggered off into movement. Eventually the whole theatre would be sealed off and anyone left inside would have no hope of escape. Some skeptics not far off were complaining that they expected more, or at least something different. Not all ran for the doors and stairs. Some continued watching moving images on a giant screen. Some people were falling, but could return to the stairs and have time to escape. My companion and I were late, but we managed to find a wall with hooks and foot holds embedded at regular intervals in the chalky wall. My companion found his way safely into a hole about thirty inches in diameter. With some difficulty I arrived at the hole and a hand in the darkness pulled me in. There were many more behind me that wanted to follow us.

May 26 1977

I was in a house whose surroundings were unfamiliar to me. Suddenly the earth trembled; an earthquake was happening. When it stopped I went about doing something, and then it started again. This time the earth opened up in front of the house. Part of the ceiling fell on me and I lost consciousness momentarily. When I awoke I realized I was alright. I went to another part of the house and noticed it was sunnier. I sat by a bay window and felt safer there. The moments that past were uneventful so I went into the living room and joined my mother-in-law and father-in-law. Through the window I could see the sun setting over the horizon.

Unexpectedly, the sun reversed its celestial direction and noticeably rose back into the sky. In the mean time, my father-in-law, who seemed to have lost a lot of weight, was scurrying about the house while I was proclaiming that it was the 'End Times'. Through all this I kept an eye on the growing sun even as I moved from one room to another. Then I had the distinct impression that the sun was coming closer to the window, it did not increase in size. There was a sense of divinity in the orange glow. Droplets of light fell from the melting sun and landed on the heads of monkeys. I had no idea where they were coming from, but they were coming endlessly by the hundreds and thousands and covering their eyes and faces with their hands as they did so. They seemed to be nourished by the sun and there was a certain kind of radiance about their heads.

The sun hovered in front of my window like a heavenly star ship. I went down on my knees. I felt that I understood everything. I turned my head, with my eyes closed, to the right at a sixty degree angle away from the presence of the sun. Still I was able to look at the sun with the left side of my head. I was in a state of deep reverence. I was walking on my knees all over the floor. Life was manifest in everything. A four and a half foot tall African statue made of ebony walked across the floor to open the front door and someone walked in. Plants were emitting blissful consciousness. All these events occurred as though quite natural. Everything was aware of everything. The flaming sun evoked a sense of deepest awe and wonder; there was celebration in sacred color. Evolution was stepped up to revolution.

Circa 1975

I was in a dark wooded region running away from someone. I came to a building and went inside. I walked down hallways with many doors in what seemed like an old office building. As I wandered through the building I finally came to a door and heard a voice say, "This is the one." So I opened the door and stepped into the brightness outside. Before me was a smooth green lawn and in the distance I could see trees. After walking across the lawn and arriving at the trees I turned around and looked toward the building only to see a very tall wall. As I gazed upon the wall I could make out a clear image as though I was watching a movie. I could see a giant green apple. It was a very vibrant florescent green full of life. Someone beside me asked what I saw and I described the apple. Then he said look closer, deeper. I noticed a reflection of a window on the apple and as I looked inside I could make out a city. Looking still further I could see a street corner. The next thing I new, I was standing on the street corner and looking up, to my amazement, I could see many different types of bicycles moving through the air. They were assorted in color, flying with ease about fifteen to twenty feet above the ground. Some bikes had four or more seats and would bend as they turned in the sky. I stood there gazing at this marvelous spectacle until I woke up.

March 12 1972

I was in a snow covered landscape somewhere near the Arctic Circle. I found myself sitting and observing in the back of a sled while a musher was directing the dog team. In the distance I could see other dog teams and sleighs. Nothing unusual was going on except that our speed was gradually increasing. A sense of excitement started to swell within me as we started lifting off the ground. I held on firmly as we rose higher and more rapidly. The other dog teams could be seen far below as we ascended. I could make out the roundness of the planet on the horizon. At a certain point in time, the driver, the dogs and the sleigh were gone. The Earth shrunk from view. The sun became so distant that I could not tell it apart from any of the other stars across the universe, and still I kept rising. By now this ascension was expressing itself differently. The twinkling stars were condensing and replacing the darkness with a blanket of light. Billions of points of light were now within me and all around me. I could clearly hear an all knowing voice resounding like an echo throughout and within, "Being One, Being One."

There was no separation from the voice and the actual state I was in. I was everything and everything was me. I had the impression that my Earthly body was far below and wanted this conscious moment to go on forever but the experience evaporated as I awoke. When I closed my eyes to recall the state I had just left behind, my memory of the details were fresh and clear.

April 15 1971

PART 1

It was 5:30am, downtown. The streets were empty and the buildings were tall. Dawn's soft glow of light threw long shadows but the sun in the sky was black.

PART 2

In this next scene I was still downtown but the buildings were smaller. A biker was kicking someone on the ground. Then he mounted his bike and started driving in circles. The motor was encased in a small container made of thin walls and the wheels appeared to be slender. He was saying, "Man, he should have known, anything, but he shouldn't mess around with a biker's bike!"

PART 3

Next, I was sitting behind a friend on a bike and I was just about to tell him to take it easy when he accelerated the throttle and we lifted off the ground. We rose quickly and I was struck with wonder as we moved over florescent green and yellow clouds. These clouds went as far as the horizon; the sky was also florescent green but lighter than the clouds. There were two other bikers riding ahead to the left of us. Slowly the clouds dispersed and the sun rose in the sky. The other bikers descended. We continued riding in exhilaration until, not long after, I awoke.

December 13 1970

After much chase and excitement, I found myself in an elevator. I had a moment of peace and as the elevator went up I became aware I was dreaming. I suddenly realized I had never slept in an elevator. As I proceeded to put myself into a deeper sleep, the elevator moved more rapidly. I remained as quiet as I could, remembering that I had been in similar situations in past dreams. By being passive but alert I hoped to have an extraordinary experience, and every indication that it would be so was there. As I was rising faster and faster the ceiling was transforming into a starry sky. But I could not maintain my inner quiet and woke up.

Summer 1969

It was dark and windy and I just came back from a mission with a submarine located in a harbor with dark waters. On my way home I realized I forgot something important on the submarine, so I turned around and ran back as fast as I could. Then along side a towering fence I spotted an old man dressed in rags begging for money. I felt I had a good excuse to ignore him so I continued running but he cried out in desperation and I couldn't go on. Returning to the beggar, I emptied my pockets of all my coin and offered it to him. Then, without a warning the clouds broke up and bright light came flooding down from the sky. I turned to the light and I could hear the unmistakable voices of angels chanting. Without opening my mouth a voice within me rose up to the harmony. It was blissful. Each time my voice found a higher harmony there would be one higher than mine. I reached notes I never thought possible and it seemed like we could go on for ever doing this beautiful music. In this intensity it occurred to me that the beggar was nowhere to be seen. It was also very soon that I gently awoke to a sun filled room. I stayed still, quietly closing my eyes. I could still hear the voices in the distance within.

Dream Segments

The following segments of dreams were not written down as they occurred. Consequently they do not have accompanying dates or great detail. They have all occurred between 1970 and 1990 (give or take a year).

SEGMENT 1

It was dark. I came to a small body of dark water and although I could not see it, I knew there was an island and on that island there was a baby bear. For some reason unknown to me I had to kill the cub. I swam toward the island but halfway there I was gripped by some unseen force and pulled back away from the island. I was afraid and resisting the force was useless.

SEGMENT 2

Crossing a downtown city street, I felt as though I was under the influence of a hallucinogenic drug. The road was shifting and moving like the waves of an ocean. The sidewalk curb was about fifteen feet high.

SEGMENT 3

In the distance we could make out a wall about twice the size of a man. I was walking with George Harrison of the Beatles across a big smooth lawn. He was telling me the meaning of some of the lyrics in Beatle songs. He said, "Sergeant Pepper, when pronounced very quietly, was the sound of cosmic waves."

SEGMENT 4

I was in a room watching two televisions. One emitted predominantly blue light and the other, red. I was able to split my attention between the two and indeed this was the aim of the entertainment. The screens were made of hundreds of glass discs which were meant to be added and removed as part of the entertainment. Under each disc removed, there was a smaller disc but the surface of the screen somehow remained constantly smooth. . Adding and removing these discs gave the effect of experiencing different types of clarity which in turn affected the emotional experience of the program.

SEGMENT 5

I was pointing out the juxtaposition of an atom in a rusty bolt and an atom in my body, thus making an invisible link between the two atoms. There are billions of atoms in the bolt and billions in my body. In the world of atoms there are billions to the power of billions, which was an insight in the microcosm.

Poetry

M

I lost the letter after L
I searched all over but could not find her
I looked under T
She was not there
I looked after Zee
But A was there
I checked everywhere
Then noticed a double W
So I turned one over
And there she was, M!

This Poem is Easy to Read

Not every line will rhyme
However, it will this time
If I have something to say
I hope it has meaning for you
If I have insights to share
I hope you share them too
If I dream of a wonderful place
It wouldn't be without you
If nothing else, you must agree
This poem was easy to read

The Funnel

downward dark impos sibledepre sssadness
fearchaosc onfusion disa rraydisorder
muddleanarchy discord tumult tur
moil upheavalclutteredbed lam
riot messsin pand emo
nium troubleno
shoutstress
wo rry
miser
yidle
cant
spo
il
o
ve
can
will
sa ve
g race
an swer
guru art
fabulo us
tru ebe ing
divi n ecalm
oneho nest go od
univer sal ligh ttrust worthy
thereisalwayslightattheendofthefunnel

He Looked Like Ringo

He looked a lot like Ringo
But I know if Ringo was he
I'd recognize him right away
Because he looks exactly like him

Part 1 (part 1)

A second is like an hour
An hour is like a day
A day is like a week

Part 1 (part 2)

A week is like a day
A year is like a day
A lifetime is like a day
A week of lifetimes is like a day
A year of lifetimes is like a day
A lifetime of lifetimes is like a day
A day is like an hour
An hour is like a second

Part 2

How to ponder the life span of a micro cosmic being

Gratitude

(In memory of G. I. Gurdjieff)

You left so many years ago
So many years ago you said good bye

I don't know where you are
Where you are is a mystery

If now you were here
I could only wish to be here now

Your teaching is like a road map
A map that guides me through this life

With my friends I think of you
I think of you in gratitude
For all you found and shared
The world is richer because of you

And so in body and spirit now and here
I wish you joy always everywhere.

To Be

to be two
entities

what is chance
time and space

you see you
see me see

together
forever

discover
each other

understand
we can work

unlock doors
we can play.

Will a simple
Twist of fate
Overshadow
Miracle?

Two be or not Two be

We be two entities
Passing in time
The chance is
We see each other
Holding together in love
Can we work together?
Can we discover each other?
Can we understand each other?
Can we unlock doors forever?

Will a simple twist of fate
Unlock the miracle
For us to be?

Camera Talk

the negative road and sidewalks
race up the edge of buildings.
masses of dull colors
framing beautiful people
walking the poisonous street.
lovers hand in hand
licking tongues and ice cream.
food shops, bright lights-
frame this girl, crop that crowd.
how many heavenly faces
pass by, not knowing, not seeing?

i'd like to Peel off Saint Catherine Street,
roll it up
and send it off for developing.
all my prisoners would bathe in chemicals
until forms would appear,
contacting with a stop to the light…
exposed!

all those people – all those frames.
another message slips off deaf ears
and gets sucked into the moon.

you're not really doing,
everything is happening.

The Green Swan As Far As The Eye Can See

Once upon a time there was a peculiar green
  swan with quaint silver spectacles sitting in a cozy
    armchair reading a delightful book by a warm fireplace in
      a charming room in a country house nestled between an old forest and
        rolling hills as far as the eye can see.

She was reading a story about a magical swan that happened to be
  green but could look like a bear when she ventured in dreams
    to far away places where waters run deep
      beneath dark and strange islands forgotten beyond
        rolling hills as far as the eye can see.

The bear was a cub that moved in dark places roaming in shadows of mystery
  where time was no more and spaces lay empty
    looking for children she wished to set free
      to lead them from nightmares back to the happy
        rolling hills as far as the eye can see

Through valleys, over hilltop, children followed in glee,
  those that feared were bathed in peace, sadness would give way
    to joy, those that worried danced in elation
      all the way back to the house between an old forest and
        rolling hills as far as the eye could see.

And there they came by the hundreds of thousands
  to sit by the warm fire place in the room
    where the peculiar green swan sat reading her book
      to these children who had just come from the
        rolling hills as far as the eye can see.

The Green Swan As Far As The Eye Can See (continued)

She was reading a story about a cub that was on a dark island
  where dark waters run deep, in a lightless ebony land and there came a
    stranger whose purpose it was to murder her for no reason.

The cub, knowing this, waited and as the killer entered the water
  swimming, the magical cub summoned the queen of the seven swans
    and bade her "to charm this one for he knows not what he is doing."

So 'the queen of the heavens and the world' drew him backwards away from the
  island, with a swift and invisible force, pounding his heart with fear
    and diverting him from the secret of the green
      swan who lives in a country house between an old forest and
        rolling hills as far as the eye can see.

The green swan now grew tired of tales and so removed her silver spectacles
  and stirred all the children to awaken,
    as she fell quietly asleep in her cozy armchair by a warm fireplace
      in a charming room in a country house nestled between an old forest and
        rolling hills as far as the eye can see.

Black Swan 2

It seems like yesterday
This old box I found
Of silver and of broken glass
Crystal clear and red
Welded with lead
Velvet inside and scented cedar
Where later I put things
Where I found
A black swan folded
Downtown
A picture of rush hour
Tumbling from the sky – bricks
Heavy from above – no water
Liquid ripples unfolding
A black swan downtown
Rush hour – no water
Bricks crashing all around
The black swan alone - naive
Eyes upon the falling bricks
Danger hit her gentle wing
Motionless, down on my knee
Gazing through camera eye
watch her flee
her spirits fouled…
But I didn't find the box
until many hears later
at that point in time
I decided to place that photograph
Of the black swan with its red wing
Into it
Along with
My picture of the yellow cow
The crystal snail
The ancient coins

And the original poem
Of the black swan.
Of course, since then
The box has filled up
With many interesting things
This is why the box is old
Because I found this box
Many many years ago
Although it seems like yesterday.

Wrapped in the hide of the Yellow Cow

Revolution
Lake over fire
Clinging below the joyous
When the time is right you will be believed
Now is the time of transformation
A leaf does not change its color in a day
A caterpillar does not a butterfly become over night
A government takes time to hear the people
Yellow is the color of the middle
The cow is gentle
The man who brings change makes glad the people
First within yourself
Then throughout the world.

Many Interesting Things

You see,
This little wooden box
Was carved from the same cedar
As imagination.
So, no matter how many things
I put into it
There is always room for more.
Therefore I did not want to put anything.
I chose many interesting things!
Things such as The Secret
Of the Blue Ridge Mountain Queen's
Red Swan Part 3 on digital vellum,
Which like the time fax machine,
will be invented later.
　　　　I know All About It,
　　　　But It is not in this poem.
In this poem, you will find out about
Many interesting things;
The ability to fly without benzene
Why anyone is alive,
Especially you.
How secrets are hidden
When answers are given.
The structure of sound and image projectors
One thousand years from now.
The meaning of expanding
The inner sanctum sanctorum.
The purpose of animals
In stories of dreams and nature,
Beneath the billions
Of stars around us
On this space ship
We call the Solar System.

All about It

Well! Here It is.
It is what It is.
But sometimes It is more.
Whatever It is,
We have to deal with It right now.
Or not!
Now It's here
Later It's gone
Later is now
So now It's gone
Later It's here
What is It?

Oh - It's OK.
Oh - It's not OK.
It's a lady
Her name is Miss Leading
It's this and that.
It's in another poem.
But It wasn't in That poem.
That one was about Many Interesting Things.
I hope you found it interesting!
What I found illuminating about It
Was that It could be anything,
And It could be nothing.

Other Things in the Box

You may recall mention of photos
In an old box
Well, the photos were old
But not the only things in the box
There was also another box in the old box
But smaller
In fact
The size of a match box
In fact it was colored
It had a pretty design like flowers made by a nine year old girl
With the word love on it
Apart from that, a champagne cork
Popped in mirth in honor of
The first time we shared it;
My wife's birthday, that is,
Immediately after meeting at our favorite park
Where she showed me interesting
Pictures of her and her
Family in Italy
This was before we ever made love
So I took six
And put them into my box
Beside my little box
Which I took out
And showed her.
She opened the little box
She saw sea shells.
She put them in her hand.
These shells were from
Somewhere by the sea;
That's why they were called sea shells.
She put them back
Into the box with love
Which she put on a black wing dripping blood

Beside the cow
Wrapped in a yellow hide
Covering the hunter
Mentioned in the original poem
Of the black swan.

The Original Poem of the Black Swan

A few years ago
In the mountains of Italy
I met an old man dressed in rags
A storyteller
Begging for money
I stopped to give him some

He started to talk
His words lured me into a trance
A curse
It weighed me down
A tale of doom unwound
A chilling tale of gloom
I thought of leaving-
Ah, but one more word
And then another
And what would be said
After the other.
The more he spoke
The more he spoke
I dream I
In the eye of the hurricane
Succumbed.

As I recall
There was a swan
As black as night
Enchanted
Never to have flight
Years ago in virgin wood
She moved through shadows
And through time

Searching for the secret that would set her free
From the bane that was upon her.
And so one day she came, astray
Upon a place where farmers dwell.
The hunter with his loaded gun
Saw the bird and then took aim...
They were poised in a conflict of interest.
She made to flee but was grazed by the fence
Moving rather hastily in self defense
She all dressed all beautiful all black
Except the red blood dripping down her back...

The storyteller paused
To warn me of my fate
If I listen any more
Then I must take his weight
I must take his tattered clothes
And assume his age
I must beg in paradise
And endure the rain
For no roof will shelter me
Nor a woman comfort me
No harbor for my ship at sea
No peace to ever set me free
Know peace – I said to me
Try to be free
Had to shrug off the hypnosity
I jolted away

I turned my back to the storyteller
And cut myself as I stumbled and fell
With wings of fear I flew from there
To see him never more.

Red Swan

$$\Pi$$
aM
embryO
fire red swaN
peculiar attributE
as mystical as greek pI
as venerated as isiS
my aunt victoriA
her red shawL
being in alL
puzzling I
red seA
i aM
$$\Pi$$

Aunt Victoria's Fire Engine Red Shawl

Un-be-lee-va-bull!
One-Ballet-in-a-bubble
So delicate my aunt Victoria
With her fire engine red shawl
The shawl had peculiar properties
The peculiar properties embraced her
Then it stirred moving gracefully down
Slipping seductively settling to the ground
Red was the ground as the red swan rose
Rose through the window into the blue
Blue fades from red fades to black
Black transforms to bubble
bubble in a buballet
Unbelievable!

The Secret of the Blue Ridge Mountain Queen's Red Swan (Part 2)

Recently (no more that ninety five years ago, I'm sure)
I journeyed South to the Blue Ridge Mountains
Seeking out the little silver faeries
(Or so the song goes)
Nevertheless hello
To a place I did go
Where I might find this magic folk.

I did not search and search and search
Where endless is the word
But wait nearby a crystal stream
Beneath a massive tree
Not high high high
But high enough
With many branches branching
And every leaf on every twig
A splendor to be holding.

Someone shifted right beside me
Clad in camouflage
Someone sighed, it wasn't me
Someone tall as I
Fine and noble
Sly and wise
With a twinkle
In his eyes

He spoke to me
In clandestine
And chanting tongue
Of faerie queen
And seven diamonds
In a crown

A certain scepter
Pungent saffron
Winds that twirl
Around the world
Raiment rustle
On the ground
Made of silk
Maiden swan.

The Time Capsule

In a protected region
On the day he celebrated his birthday
Thirty three year old Hunter Swanson
Found a time capsule
Dated June 11 2026
In the grass lands of the Arctic Circle.

To his lab in his home
Did he bring from the past
This amazing millennium
Travelling quest.
Releasing the lock
To find something within
He caressed it and smelled it
After pulling it out.
It was hard wood and smooth
Smelled like cedar should
Transfixed before treasure
Giving in to temptation
What mysteries hide
In this messenger of time

Strange coincidence that it was
Engraved on the side to give him pause
A date exactly the date it was found
But a thousand years ago to date

Could it be somehow
The sender knew
The great white north
Would no longer be,
That someone like Swanson
Would stumble upon
Something so curious
As what he stumbled upon

Swanson looks and sees inside
Antiquities forgotten
Colored photos
Wrinkled and folded
Swans never been seen
Black red blue and green.

Swanson fumbles for the other box
As tiny as a shell
He sees love on it
He takes a look inside
An ocean breeze fresh and clean
As what it must have been
Many many years ago
Now fills his nostril dream
On and on this magic scent
Plays inside his head
Until he slowly closes
This little lovely box.

There beside the box with love
A snail of crystal scattered light
Upon three ancient coins,
The likes of which
Date back two thousand
Years or maybe more.

Inscribed with writing from the East
This currency of bronze
Possessed a hole
But the hole was square.
The money was bound with leather strap
From the hide of a yellow cow
The strap in turn was bound by wood
Quite possibly bamboo.

Many items found therein
Fascinated him

For hours he would gaze upon
One thing and another
Until he came upon the matter
That puzzled like no other.

Crumpled up into a ball
Was a document
Obsolete material
Obscure and fragile
Although digital vellum is obsolete
How did it come to be
Locked inside a capsule dated
Twenty twenty six
Since digital vellum was invented in
Twenty eighty six
That ancient English spoken then
Is hard do comprehend
And to make the matter worse
The text is stained and rent
Coffee blots mixed with ink
Analysis revealed
Pieces torn and parts burned
Tears are evident
Though digital vellum was a substance strong
A thousand years is very long

For days and nights he labored long
To comprehend the text
With every word that was revealed
The mystery perplexed.

Anyways – to make a long poem short
Turn to The Secret of the Blue Ridge
Mountain Queen's Red Swan
(Part 3) in a Time Capsule,
Where you will find
The Synopsis of It!
Dates and clues to the Time Fax Machine
Will be included.

The Secret of the Blue Ridge Mountain Queen's Red Swan (Part 3) in a Time Capsule

The Synopsis of It

The following poem   is   the version found
in a time capsule   by Hunter Swanson
The capsule dates   back to June 11 2026
It was found   exactly   one thousand year later
To the day;   that day also being
Hunter Swan-   son's birthday
A photocopy of   the original document
Was faxed to me   by a fully compatible
Time-fax machine   which will be invented
Much later but   which doesn't matter
Anyway, because   it's fully compatible.
Even as I write,   it   is June 11, 2011
But this   can change!
Due to the condition of   the poem found in the capsule,
It was difficult   to decipher
And it was only through   Mr. Swanson's help
That I found   the original poem
Which I transmitted   to him in a dream.

The Time Fax Machine

The Time Fax Machine is not made of plastic
Not of screws and washers
It has no moving parts
It is much more sophisticated

You will not find it at a mall
Don't look for it in an office
It is not under a bench or in a hall

Write your letter to the dead
And take it with you to your bed

Invent it in your sleep to send it in a dream.

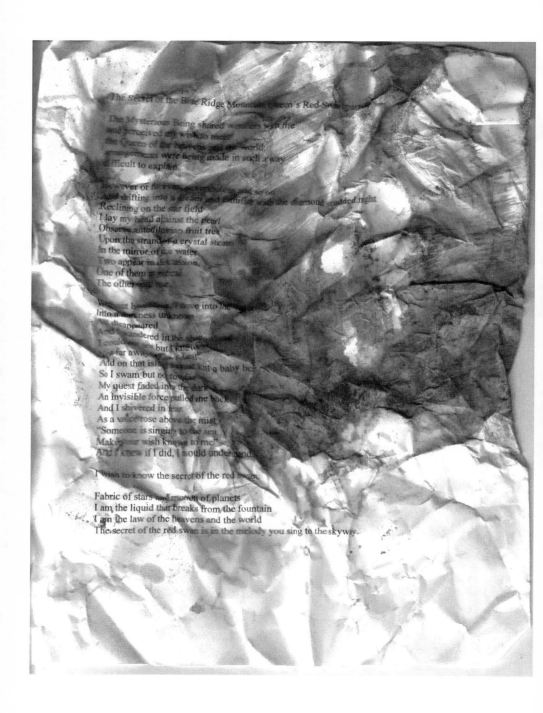

The Secret of the Blue Ridge Mountain Queen's Red Swan

The Mysterious Being shared wisdom with me
and perceived my wish to meet
the Queen of the heavens and the world;
arrangements were being made in such a way
difficult to explain.

However or forever, something was set to
And drifting into a galaxy and familiar with the diamond studded night
Reclining on the star field
I lay my head against the pearl
Observe antediluvian fruit tree
Upon the strands of a crystal stream
In the mirror of the water
Two appear in discussion,
One of them is me
The other one was

Without hesitation, I dove into the water
Into a darkness unknown
And disappeared
And I wandered in the shadow
I could not see but I knew
So far away, on the island
And on that island sweet but a baby bee
So I swam but not toward
My quest faded into the dark
An invisible force pulled me back
And I shivered in fear
As a voice rose above the mist
"Someone is singing to the sea
Make your wish known to me"
And I knew if I did, I would understand

I wish to know the secret of the red swan

Fabric of stars and motion of planets
I am the liquid that breaks from the fountain
I am the law of the heavens and the world
The secret of the red swan is in the melody you sing to the skyway.

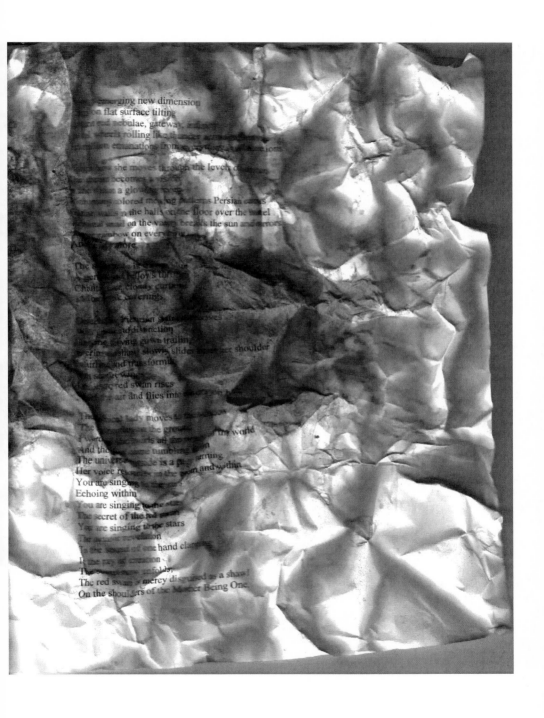

...emerging new dimension
...on flat surface tilting
...red nebulae, gateway...
...wheels rolling like thunder around...
...motion emanations from mythology...

...now she moves through the levels of...
...dream becomes a vision
...are within a glowing temple
...many-colored flowing patterns Persian rugs
...walls in the halls on the floor over the water
...small on the water breaks the sun and across...
...rainbow on every...
And there more...

The sun... on the throne...
...her... like Allah's little...
Chanting... cloudy curtains...
all billowing, coverings...

...Persian sultan moves...
...poem and distraction
...flowing flowing gown trailing...
...flowing slowly slides over the shoulder
...swirling and transform...
...in slowly winds...
...red swan rises
...art and flies into...

The... lady moves to the...
The... the greatest... the world
...words... all over... the world
...and the... come tumbling down
The universe inside is a poem turning.
Her voice resounds in the poem and within
You are singing to the stars
Echoing within...
You are singing to the stars
The secret of the red swan
You are singing to the stars
The inner revelation
In the sound of one hand clapping...
In the ray of creation...
The... unfolds,
The red swan - mercy disguised as a shawl
On the shoulders of the Master Being One.

The Dream Traveler

I was walking through a field of tall grass
Sensing there was an object that I could not see
Keeping very still an opening appeared
So I approached to see what was inside

Now I knew it was a ship to travel space
And there before me I see an open door
Clearly I could make out Beatle records
In a room as warm as home

Making my way inside to a couch
With no surprise I sat before a very gentle man
Who handed me a large shiny container
And he began to speak

Father, I have journeyed through time and dream
To bring back this trove found in this casing
A poem you wrote or perhaps will write
For which I obsess to have understanding

I am not your father I told him.
I do not know you; I have no children
But dared did I to look inside
And find this ragged old parchment

I come from the future where this object I found
Your name was on it, you see, it is there
It was true what he said, my name and a date
Though the date was to come only some time later

It was then that I realized this was a dream
And I said to myself I know I am dreaming
I said 'I know this is a dream'
See your self, he said, you are everything.

So I pulled out a snail made from fine crystal
Given to me by an old man from Rochetta
Although almost blind, with this crystal snail
He could see dancing lights like the ones in Eureka

Without touching a thing I knew that within
Painted with love, a small and light box
Containing shells, ribbons and fragrance divine
And multi colored swans gathered in flocks

I saw coins and books and leather straps
Bamboo and cedar and a mirror too
I picked up a black swan with a red wing
Turned over the photo to read something

Look through the snail make your eyes crystal clear
I pondered until my attention was trapped
By the fish on the floor wriggling to disappear
But the fish was weak so I brought it to water

I sank into a bath and ate another fish
I turned to where gardens hung and more jewels swam
As water cools it brims with kaleidoscope angels
And tropical wonders; the beach curled with sea shells

Infinite patterned sand design, every grain a universe
Every star a grain of sand, I stepped out of the water
And moved across the star field
Came out of the little box with love and closed it

And placed it there beside the snail
In the cedar box upon the mantle shelf
Folded the photo into my wallet
And listened to the voice of the traveler

Keep this secret for a while wrapped in the hide of a yellow cow
The ancient coins will serve you well when summoning the oracle
His voice was tender much like my father's
His voice was sweet much like my daughter's

Make these answers into questions
Wake up poets in their dream
Discover treasures in the heart
Of s/he who struggles to be free

Put them in a cedar box
On a bed of velvet
Beneath the velvet place a mirror
With nothing and yourself in it

Make these treasures mystery
Wrap them up poetically
Perform them well and you will see
Fame and fortune at you feet

Let splendor kiss the eyes that see
And meaning fill the open ear
Let your simple words free
Those who cloak their life in fear

Fold them all inside a box
Neatly by the sea
Put it all inside this tube
Addressed to destiny

Don't let the Beatles fool you
They know more than what they let on
But that's alright you'll find out more
If you listen to their song

Leave the package by the PEARL
Under the midnight sun
Where old winds make cold snow swirl
And daylight skies are cinnamon

In a thousand years as a matter of fact
When the North is warm and green
I find this capsule all in tact
On Peninsula Fosheim

You must turn it in my mind
As I sleep at night
And as I meet you in your dream
You must come to mine

Using the power of silent mind
Shield yourself with non thinking
Observe what substance you're made of
You may be one and everything

So take this parchment in your dream
And welcome now into my dream
Reveal at last the secret key
To the Blue Ridge mountain queen's red swan part three

Revealing the Secret

Hunter Swanson disappeared and I was left alone
Within visible without invisible
Within a dream the ship it seemed
Invisible without, but when I dreamed inside the ship
All was visible
Except for Hunter Swanson - who was invisible.
I had a dream I fell asleep
And slept a thousand years
Into a room I floated just
Above the water floor
Into which I could see
The universe and more
I flew above the table there
And to the mantle came
And saw a picture of a man
Swanson was his name
And then it was that I recalled
That all this was a dream
I was awake – I was asleep
Yet nothing was the same
Consciousness was everything
The table, cup and walls
And far below the water floor
Asleep, my body lay
A simple wish to awake
Was all that it would take
Then I recalled the strange request
Swanson made of me
On the mantle shelf I looked
And found a wooden box
In the wooden box I found
A tiny crystal snail
I peered into the crystal snail
As far as eye could see

Rolling hills and forest green
A cabin tucked between
And by a fire in a room
A swan of feather green
Reading from a magic book
The Secret of the Blue Ridge Mountain Queen's Red Swan (part 3)

Suddenly I had the key
To turn in Swanson's dream.

The Secret of the Blue Ridge Mountain Queen's Red Swan (part 3)

The Mysterious Being shared wonders with me
and perceived my wish to meet
the Queen of the heavens and the world;
arrangements were being made in such a way
difficult to explain.

However or forever, nevertheless and so on
And drifting into a dream and familiar with the diamond studded
night
Reclining on the star field
I lay my head against the pearl
Observe antediluvian fruit tree
Upon the strand of a crystal steam
In the mirror of the water
Two appear in discussion,
One of them mystical
The other one, me.

Without hesitation, I dove into the water
Into a darkness unknown
All disappeared
And I wandered in the shadowland
I could not see but I knew
Not far away lay an island
And on that island I must kill a baby bear.
So I swam but not too far
My quest faded into the dark
An invisible force pulled me back
And I shivered in fear
As a voice rose above the mist
"Someone is singing to the sea
Make your wish known to me"
And I knew if I did, I would understand.

I wish to know the secret of the red swan.

Fabric of stars and motion of planets
I am the liquid that breaks from the fountain
I am the law of the heavens and the world
The secret of the red swan is in the melody you sing to the skyway.

Rising, emerging new dimension
Rings on flat surface tilting
Distant red nebulae, gateway, infinity
Astral wheels rolling like thunder across the heavens
Vermillion emanations from everything in all directions.

Watch how she moves through the levels of a dream
The dream becomes a vision
In the vision a glowing room
With many colored moving patterns Persian carpets
On the walls in the halls on the floor over the mantel
A crystal snail on the vanity breaks the sun and mirrors
Scatter rainbow on everything
And there's more.

The sky outside is crayon blue
A gentle wind billows through
Chantilly lace cloudy curtains
Mulberry silk coverings.

Descending Victorian stairs she moves
With grace and distinction
Her long flowing gown trailing
As crimson shawl slowly slides from her shoulder
Unfurling and transforming
With scarlet wings
A majestic red swan rises
Cracks the air and flies into the crayon blue.

The mystical lady moves to the window
The silk rustles on the ground
I watch as she twirls all the winds of the world
And the stars come tumbling down
The universe outside is a page turning
Her voice resounds in the room and within
You are singing to the stars
Echoing within
You are singing to the stars
The secret of the red swan
You are singing to the stars
The octave revelation
To the sound of one hand clapping
In the ray of creation
The secret now unfolds;
The red swan is mercy disguised as a shawl
On the shoulders of the Mother Being One.

A Split Second

Wake up
Wake up, we are dead
Until this life, for a million years were we dead
After life, for a million years will we be dead
For two million we are dead it can be said
Except for a split second
When something can be different.

What is this fleeting existence
Like water we cannot hold in our hands?
Who am I that I cannot
Realize who I am?
Why am I here, though I know
Not where I am?
What hope is there in this
Open silence?
I wish that something higher
Permeate my being
That every molecule of me be felt
That every thought be conscious
And that my feeling be sublime.

The Monk

There was once a monk in Tibet
Whose knowledge for hunger was whet
Sitting in Lotus one afternoon
Contemplating the meaning of life
But hoping that lunch would be served very soon
So as to avoid any strife
From his robe came a cell phone
For a meal was he dialing
Hello, Pizzeria Om?
Make me one with everything.

Wall Flowers

Roses are yellow
Violets are violet
Summer is coming
I have no regret

Windows are dirty
Floors need sweeping
Wall colors fading
Old flowers are weeping

Roses and violets
In gardens appealing
Like wallpaper ceiling
This garden's a peeling

The Car

I was walkin my dog late last night
Just a simple stroll under the star light
The air was crisp but not too cold
I took a deep breath and it touched my soul.

People were walkin up and down the street
Everyone looking for a lover to meet
The architecture everywhere was interestin
With curves, designs and rainbow colorin.

My dog had its nose sniffin the ground
Then she'd roll in the snow and listen for sound
We'd walk together til we got back home
She wanted some water so I gave her some.

The Archer's Dilemma

the wandering archer
reflects on his youth
his arrows were straight
and his aim was true
his purpose was clear
and his bow was firm
but time and temptation
laid slumber on him.

too much time
in trivial pursuits
looking for clues
for the right thing to do
to be an accountant
musician or monk
to have monopoly
on money or grace.

too many uniforms
no purpose – no goal
one fights for justice
one without cause
the grave man keeps digging
the sailor keeps searching
the boobs and their tubes
keep watching each other.

the string has no tension
the bow has been broken
his arrows were stolen
his aim is forgotten.

life is my bow
the string is my will
should the archer awaken
my aim be fulfilled.

Ponder This Pompous Proposition

if i stink more than you
        then i'll take a shower
but if you stink more than me
        then you must take a shower
however, if you stink more than me
        you may yet doubt that you do
so, we must abide by the opinion
        of a third person
if a third person cannot be found
        we may then settle on a fourth
now, if we both settle on a fourth
        that leaves three quarters for someone else
in retro, we have two on a fourth
        and three quarters for one
interestingly, if one went on a fourth
        we'd be left with two and three quarters
and everybody knows that one fourth
        and two and three quarters is equal to three
so either way we have a third person
        the only problem with a third person is
finding the other two thirds to complete the threesome
        granted, i may
stink more than you
        but if that were the case
no third or fourth person
        would stand close enough
to voice their opinion
        about who stinks more
me or you.

Impressions

the impression of a maple leaf on a virgin forest
the impression of a small white cloud on a blue eye
the impression of a bright yellow pencil on a child's mind
the impression of a woman's smile through a window on a man
the impression of a finger print on a detective
the impression of the day on the night
the impression of the moon on the sun
the impression of knowledge on the masses
                    of matter on movement
                    of rock on root
                    of sand on sailors
                    of life on water
                            on wind
                            on fire
                            on turning
                            on seasons
                            on being
                            on
                                    being
                            on
                                    being
                            on
                                    being
                            one

Observation of Impressions

To begin

i observe red and other colors
music and other sounds
perfume and other scents
pain and other sensations
i observe clouds and other shapes
i observe west and other directions
earth and other spheres
i observe Jorge and other people
i observe impressions and other nutritions

An Atomic Juxtaposition

My feet feel weird about walking on raisons
My feet have never experienced raisons
My feet keep each other company
I think this thing got off on the wrong foot

My ears don't hear each other
My ears have lobes
My ears are weighed down
I don't think my ears will fly away

My brains can't see each other
My brains are hidden
My brains are slow
I think!?

Characteristics

blue jeans
yellow striped shirt
checkered shirt
overhanging coat
space
a man
a woman with curly hair
business man
down the stairs
to the left of me
three more
bicycle chained to a tree
white handle bars
two business men
one was short
a crowd of about ten
a bigger crowd of twenty
five men same size
going south
one in green
a tie, glasses
a pen, a vest
a woman by herself
basket on bicycle
four women
one with handbag
one taller in long dress
one mostly talking
dispersion
two men with moustaches
one was curled
the tree is about thirty feet tall
has approximately forty to seventy leaves
three speed woman's bike

the tires and seat are black
but the bike is white
a woman in blue
looking at me through
her reflector sun glasses
as I write more
people pass by
she went north
and I man the east side
a woman in white pants
put her purse in the basket
and unlocked the chain
she has a light brown shirt
she said something to a man in his thirties
and maneuvered her bike
between a gray car and a red car
now there are only people and cars passing by
they are different in size and color
some going north
some going south
the sky is blue
and the air is hot
the same woman
with the basket on her bicycle
just passed by from north to south
raised her sun glasses to her forehead
looked east
and with a carefree smile
said something like
c'est beau
and continued out of sight.

You Can Change the World

if you imagine that you are the world,
imagine your bones are the forest
imagine your lungs are the sky and the air
imagine the blood in your veins to be rivers
imagine your mind is a high flying bird
imagine anger as earthquakes and storms
imagine love is a beautiful day
imagine your spirit reaching out to the stars
imagine that you are the world

if you imagine that your are the world,
imagine another human being.

The Sun and the Moon

Moon
Soft glow
Ocean tides rise
Going in going out
Ocean tides fall
Hard fire
Star

The Moon and the Sun

Commentary on Dreams

I sleep about seven or eight hours a day and while sleeping sometimes I dream. I understand that sleep regenerates my body but is there a purpose for dreaming? Clinical studies have been made analyzing brain activities while sleeping. In this day and age, many questions about dreams have been explored leading to conclusions well documented in books and reports easily found in book stores and on the internet. Bearing that in mind, what I offer here is simply my own personal experience along with views and insights I have gathered.

From an early age, I enjoyed flying in my dreams. As a child I would fly by imitating birds, flapping my arms up and down. I would often fly to a billboard in a field not far from where I lived. During the day I would climb the back of this billboard which was constructed and supported with wooden beams. By night, I would fly to the billboard and perch on top.

My earliest recollection of flying was of a scene I really do not understand. I believe I was still a toddler at the time. My impressions are vague but as I recall, I was very high and descending as though from outer space. I was clinging to a very large and fast flying object. It was important that I held on tight.

I regularly had dreams of flying but during my adolescence I dreamt of something out of the ordinary as compared to what I usually experienced in my sleep. I was in a field of tall grass. I was very happy in this beautiful place. Looking down I saw little fairies flying about. As I gazed upon them, the air was sprinkled with a kind of sparkling dust. The grass parted before me and immediately I found myself gently somersaulting through the divide.

Overcoming fears in life is something we must all deal with. Overcoming them in dreams seems to go hand in hand with our real life experience. As we shed our fears of things and actions in life, that same sense plays out in dreams. And as our courage grows in dreams so to does it grow in real life.

Like many children, I had a fear of snakes and dreaming about them was never pleasant. As I grew older and overcame many of my childhood fears, some kind of parallel growth occurred in my dreams. In one particular dream I recalled that I picked up a very large snake, perhaps a boa, and although I felt cautious I was not afraid. Since that time dreaming of snakes never bothered me again.

I often dreamt of water and it has always been an enjoyable experience. Sometimes I would dream of flying over rivers winding through forests, other times I would be sitting by a crystal clear pool and other times I might be frolicking in strong ocean waves. According to the website **www.dreammoods.com,** "to see water in your dream, symbolizes your unconscious and your emotional state of mind. Water is the living essence of the psyche and the flow of life energy. It is also symbolic of spirituality, knowledge, healing and refreshment. If the water is calm and clear, then it signifies that you are in tune with your spirituality. It denotes serenity, peace of mind, and rejuvenation."

On one occasion I was flying in a room around the legs of a table and chairs, which were suspended over the floor. The floor appeared to be the smooth surface of a deep body of water. Peering into the water I had the impression I was gazing at the universe and somewhere deep inside was Earth.

In another dream I stood before a pool of very dark but clean water. The waters were unknown to me or should I say they were the waters of the unknown. I had the feeling I was looking into infinity. I dove into this unknown and glided for a time under the water. A pale light appeared ahead and I emerged in what seemed to be an ancient Roman or Greek style bath house.

On the subject of flying dreams I found the following information at **www.dreammoods.com** very interesting. "Flying dreams fall under a category of dreams known as lucid dreaming. Lucid dreams occur when you become aware that you are dreaming. Many dreamers describe the ability to fly in their dreams as an exhilarating, joyful, and liberating experience.

If you are flying with ease and enjoying the scene and landscape below, then it suggests that you are on top of a situation. You have risen above something. It may also mean that you have gained a different perspective on things. Flying dreams and the ability to control your flight is representative of your own personal sense of power.

Having difficulties staying in flight indicates a lack of power in controlling your own circumstances. You may be struggling to stay aloft and stay on course. Things like power lines, trees, or mountains may further obstruct your flight. These barriers represent a particular obstacle or person who is standing in your way in your waking life. You need to identify who or what is hindering you from moving forward. It may also be an indication of a lack of confidence. You need to believe in yourself and not be afraid.

If you are feeling fear when you are flying or that you feel that you are flying too high, it may suggest that you are afraid of challenges and/or of success.

In reality, we cannot really fly, of course. Thus, such dreams may represent that which is beyond your physical limitations. In your mind, you can be anybody and do anything. Another way of interpreting flying dreams is that these dreams symbolize your strong mind and will. You feel undefeatable and nobody can tell you what you cannot do and accomplish. Undoubtedly these dreams leave you a great sense of freedom."

My flying dreams changed as I grew older. For one thing, I was more interested in dreams and discovered that through meditation I could have a different quality of experience while sleeping. Eventually I felt no need to flap my arms like a bird in order to fly. At the same time, I found the courage to fly higher and faster. Sometimes I flew to building tops ten stories high and other times I would soar to such heights that clouds far below looked very small. Going any higher meant leaving the atmosphere. A couple of times I braced myself, cleared my mind and plunged into deep space. Where I ended up was a nice surprise.

At one point I discovered that using willpower very helpful in attaining a certain goal. For instance, I was dreaming about being in an elevator, and as I recall, wishing to go higher. The wish was strong and the elevator was picking up momentum. Then the ceiling evaporated and I could see stars overhead.

In another dream, I was a passenger on a heavy jumbo airplane. Flying was sluggish. The plane could barely clear the tops of cars and it was slowly descending. At this moment I recalled a flying dream I had from the night before and simply willed the plane to rise – and it did.

One of the main hindrances I've encountered in flying dreams were telephone wires. Trying to get above them from below made me very apprehensive. They represented danger to me. Because they reappeared regularly in my dreams, one morning I put my concerns into a poem.

RUNWAY

one long black bending
car pursuing me
over gently slanting
farmland

one long limousine
carving distance

one low winged man
running down
reclining field
leaping over car
above house

seven long dangerous
wires flying
high flying fast
past electric wires
higher
too fast
too high

small town
wake up

As previously mentioned there was a period of time that I practiced meditation in relation to my dream or sleeping state. In a book called "The Adventure of Consciousness" by Satprem, Sri Aurobindo talks about a technique he used to become conscious of the fact that he was dreaming and what can be expected in this state of being. He explained that by developing 'the power of non thinking, one can come to silencing the mind thereby leaving oneself open to a higher experience. For several months I would practice my meditation for five minutes before going to sleep and upon waking would do the same. When I woke up I would remain still and keep my mind quiet. After a while, recollections of dreams would come to me. As long as I would not react or analyze, more and more of the dream images would unwind before me like a movie.

One night, after practicing this exercise for a couple of months I had an extraordinary experience. Aurobindo claimed that one state that was attainable was to be awake while the body remained sleeping and when this happens it would be possible to see "the stuff that you are really made of."

There was nothing unusual about the way my dream started. Then quite unexpectedly, I realized I was dreaming and became aware of several things simultaneously. A unique opportunity unfolded in front of me like a child alone in a candy store. With the exercises that I had been practicing in meditation over the past few months I automatically tapped into my power of non-thinking. An invisible protective force surrounded me. Nothing could penetrate this barrier to disturb my space. At the same time I knew my body was asleep somewhere down below and that I was connected to it by some kind of invisible chord. A simple wish to be back in my body was all I needed to animate it. Then the adventure began. I turned my attention to my surroundings. What I'm about to describe may sound quite ordinary but the emotion and the consciousness at that moment was anything but ordinary. In fact everything was consciousness. I was in a room and all the articles in it were consciousness, even the walls. There was a fireplace and a mantle shelf with some items on it. There was a couch, paintings and a number of other ordinary items and although these things were external everything was conscious of me and I was conscious of them. I was at once the observer in an experiment and at the same time I was the experiment. I could have gone on enjoying my observations further but I felt it necessary to reestablish contact with my body, for the sake of doing it intentionally, and so I did. The return was very smooth. There was no sense of distance or time. A simple wish and there I was. What was different this time was the fact that I didn't wake up – I was already awake. I simply returned to my sleeping body without any break in consciousness. There was no need to remember my experience. Everything was clear and as easy to remember as recalling what happened five seconds ago. It was just an uninterrupted part of my life which came back to me the way someone would remember a very happy experience.

Talking about lucid dreams once more, Aurobindo says, "First of all, ordinary dreams from the subconscious must be clearly distinguished from the experiences. Experiences are not dreams, though we have the habit of mixing up everything; they are real events in which we have shared on a particular plane; they are distinguished from ordinary dreams by their special intensity. All the events of the outer physical world, no matter how exceptional, seem pale by the side of these events; these leave a profound impression and a *more vivid* memory that any of our terrestrial memories, as though we had suddenly touched a richer mode of living – not necessarily richer in external representation or in color, which however may be of an unbelievable brilliance, but in contents. When the seeker on waking has this overbrimming impression, as of having bathed in a world charged with signs which want to say more than one thing at a time (our events of the physical world want to say only one thing at a time, rarely more) and before which it is possible to remain a long while without exhausting their meaning, so much do they seem to be charged with invisible ramifications and terraced depths; or when he has been present at or shared in certain scenes which seem infinitely more real than our physical senses, always so flat, as though they came up immediately against a hard and slightly photographic background, he will know he has had a veritable experience and not a dream."

The following quote from Wikipedia explains lucid dreaming quite clearly.

"A **lucid dream** is a dream in which the sleeper is aware that she or he is dreaming. When the dreamer is lucid, she or he can actively participate in and often manipulate the imaginary experiences in the dream environment. Lucid dreams can seem extremely real and vivid depending on a person's level of self-awareness during the lucid dream." For those interested in the subject, more can be found in Wikipedia under 'Lucid Dream' where, at the same time, other links and references are available.

Again, I would like to reiterate that attaching meanings to these dreams is not our objective. I do feel, however, that 'sleeping' doesn't necessarily have to be time lost. Is it possible to have a sense of continuity from one day to the next without that eight hour black out we call sleep? Dreams and visions while asleep can release us and give us insights into our fears, prejudices and limitations, and sometimes help us to solve problems we normally do not know how to deal with in real life. These experiences may at times give us glimpses into the 'extraordinary'. We may wake up with renewed faith in life and love or come to a new understanding of something very important to our life. Having lucid dreams where I had the sense of 'being one' as in 'one with the universe', or 'being awake in my dreams', has made my life more meaningful. By having more self awareness it is possible to bring more presence into my daily experiences in life. The idea that God is 'One' and 'Everything' at the same time makes my work of connecting with 'Everything' through 'being', very logical. Birth and death and what happens in between are only a part of the big picture. Being One is Being All. Sweet lucid dream!

Squibbles

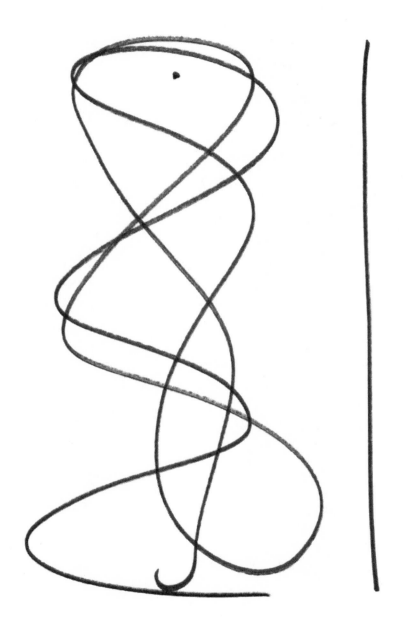

If you have a problem talking to yourself,
try talking to the wall.

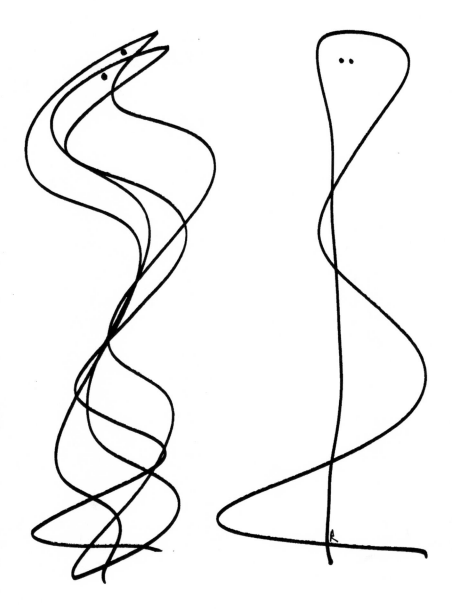

What makes you think
you're so different?

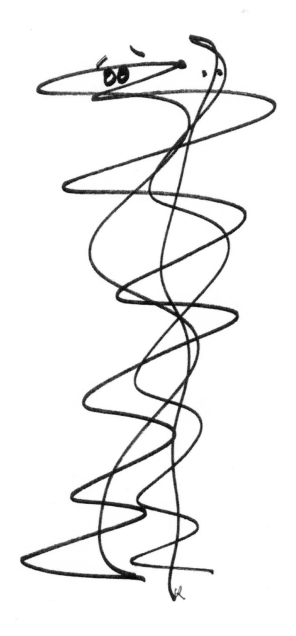

A woman likes kissing a man all over,
Until it's all over!

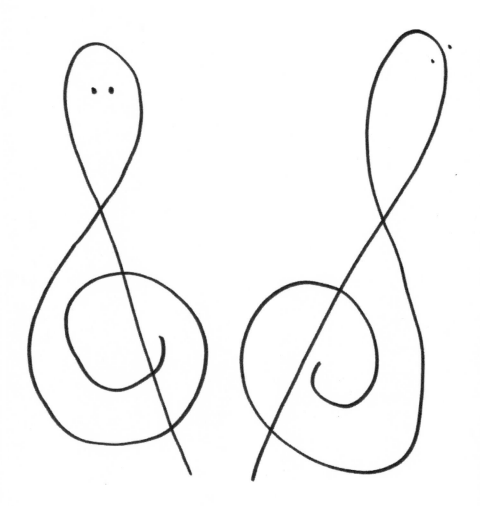

Life is a Sympathy

A bird in hand is better in the bush

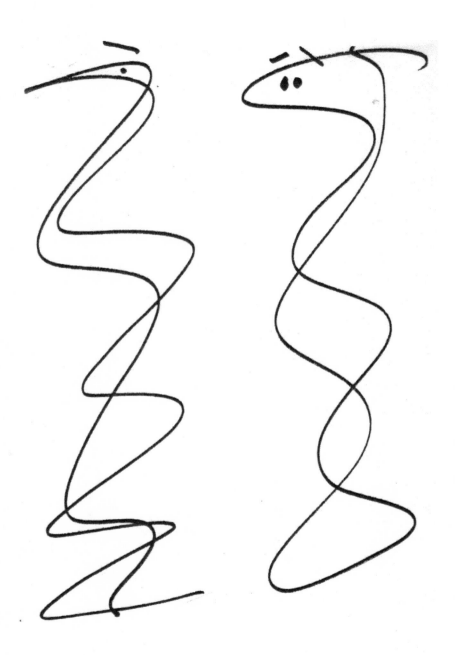

To forgive is to forget!
To forget this is unforgivable.

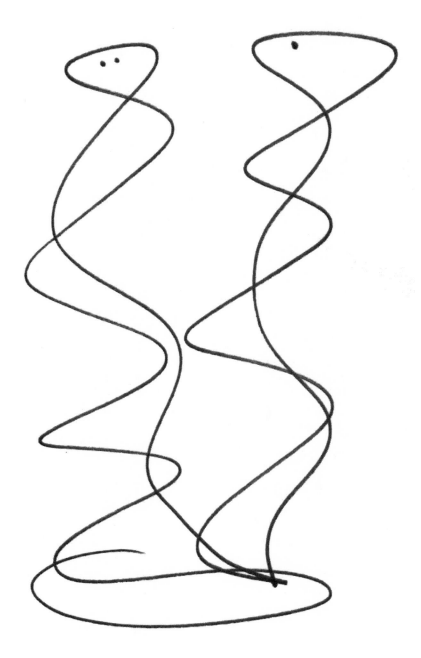

Some would like to have the answer
on a silver platter.
Others would simply prefer the silver platter.

Blessed are the poor because
that way we can get cheep labor

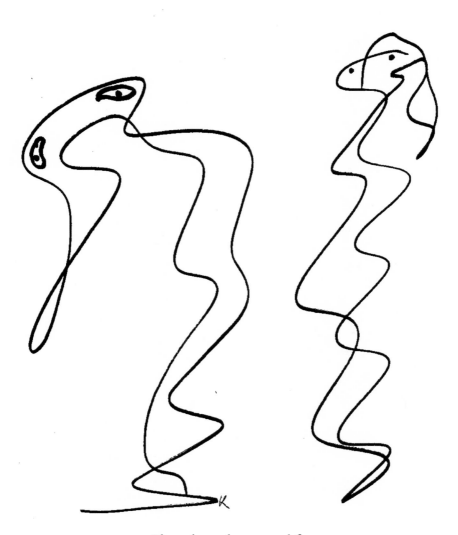

Blessed are the warped for
they know not what they know not

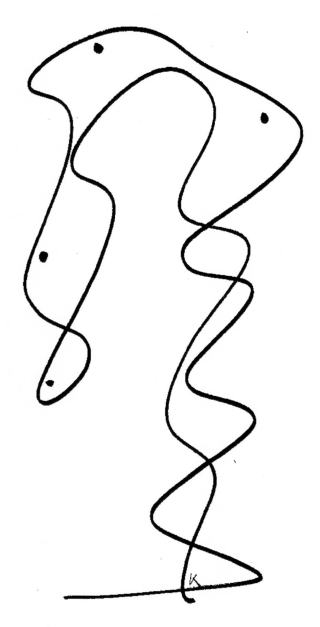

Blessed are the twisted
for being like that

Blessed are the weird
for to be one is odd

Two heads are better than one,
But one looks better

Data Overlord

Some day you're gonna make a man
A very happy woman

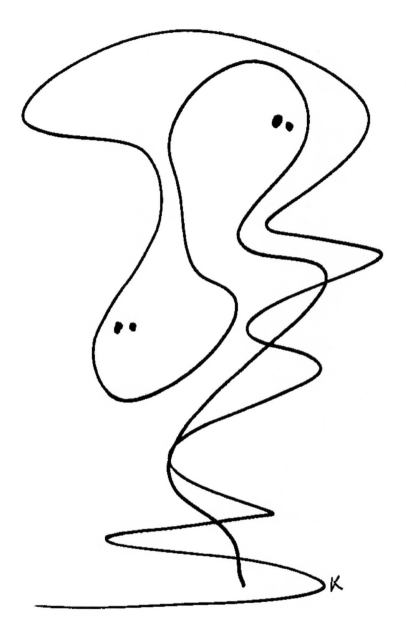

Tis better to have love and lust
Than never to have lust at all

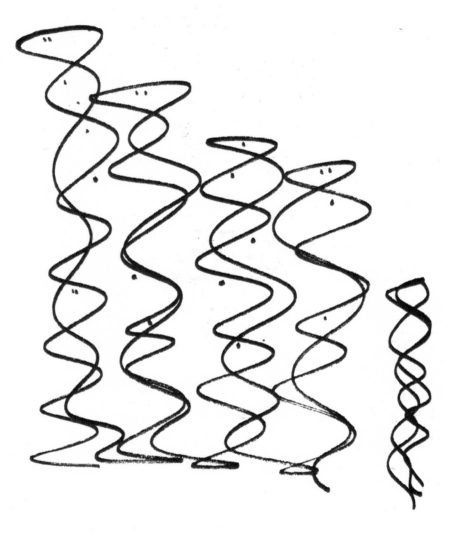

A little too much can sometimes make you wish
you had none

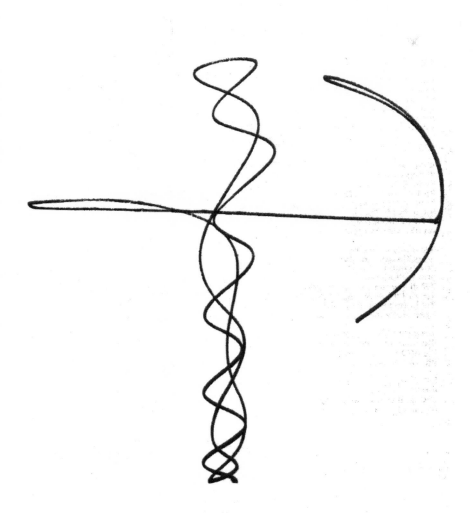

The aimless archer

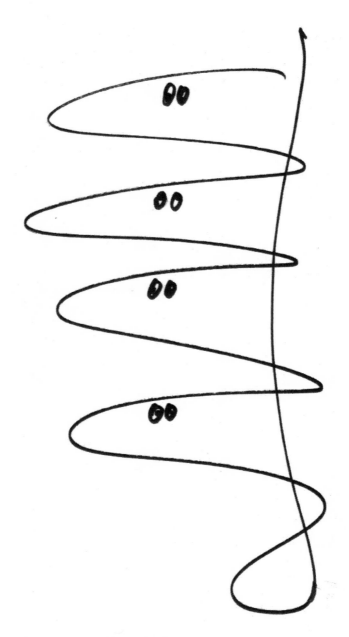

In time there is a race;
One thing is certain;
We all make the finish line.

For those trying to get ahead in life,
Check above the shoulders

Seeing is not believing!
Ask any blind man.

Someone is talking about your back
Behind you

They say you can't see the forest for the trees.
Maybe I just don't see the big picture!

Squibbles love each other
When they feel that
They don't have to love each other.

If you don't get the point,
why bother?

Where are you going?
I'm going to Seattle.
I didn't ask you who you were going to see!

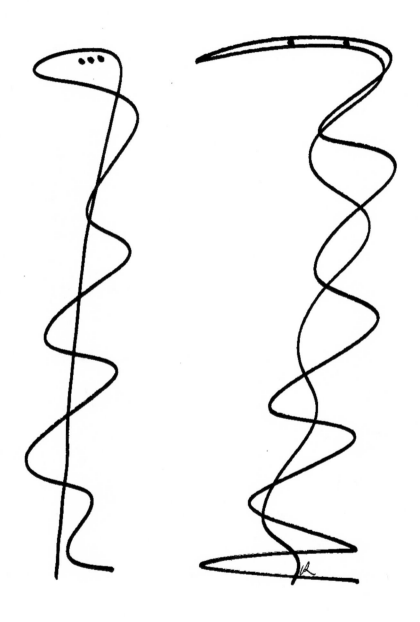

So...what did the optometrist say?

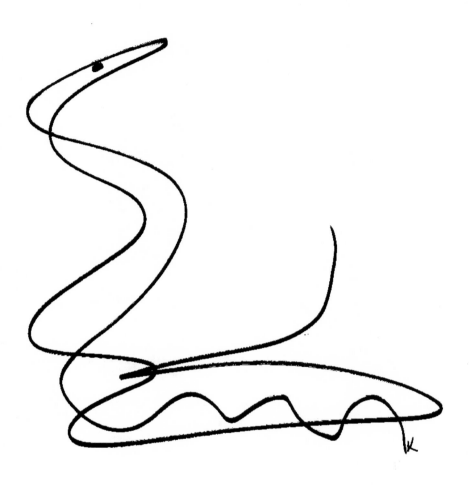

Is it a birdie?
Is it an eagle?
No!
It's par for the coarse!

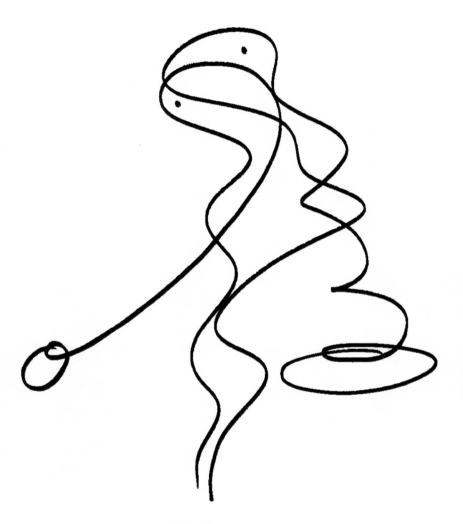

One hand is laden with 24 carats
The other with 24 hours

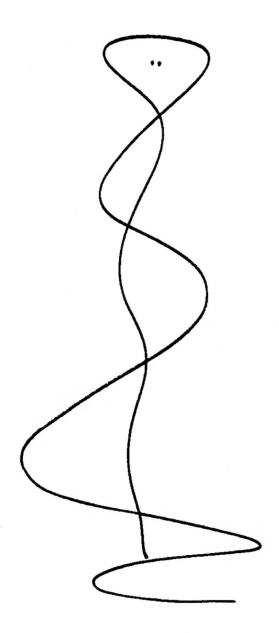

All I ever do
Is worry about my figure

We spend too much time not thinking
About how we waste our time

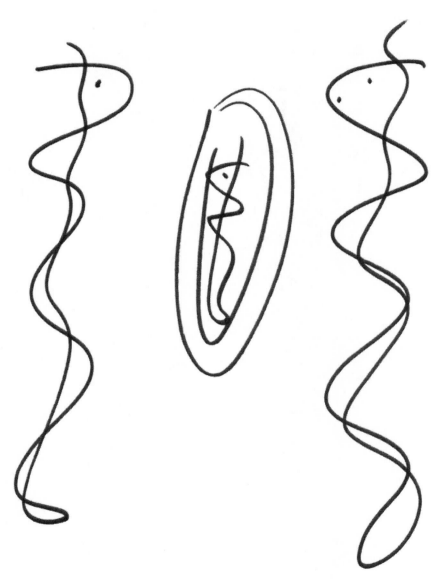

I hope your mirror doesn't come between us.

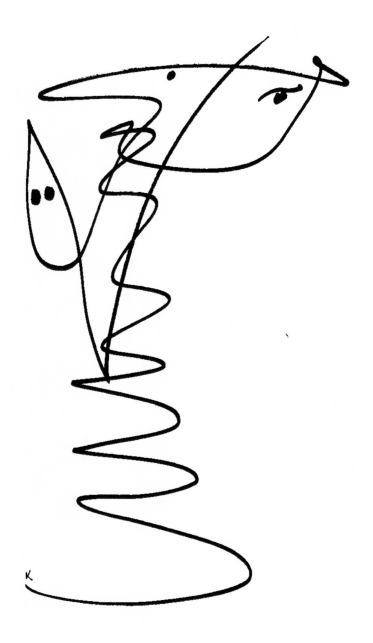

Some are two faced and some are three

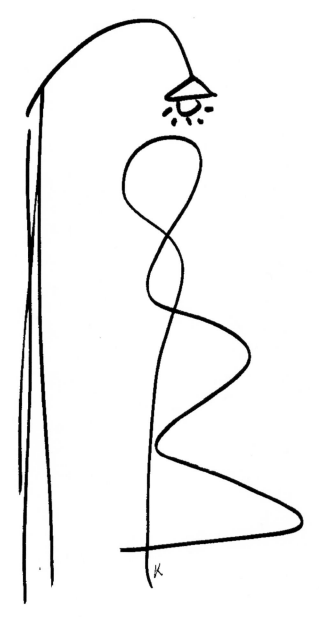

Why do we linger under a light
That will eventually burn out

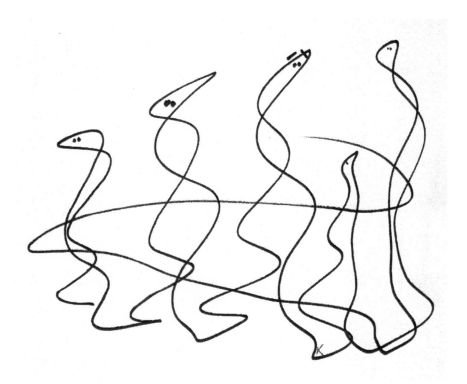

Oh shit! You mean we all got screwed

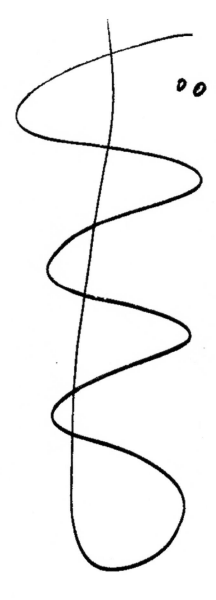

Mind Grip

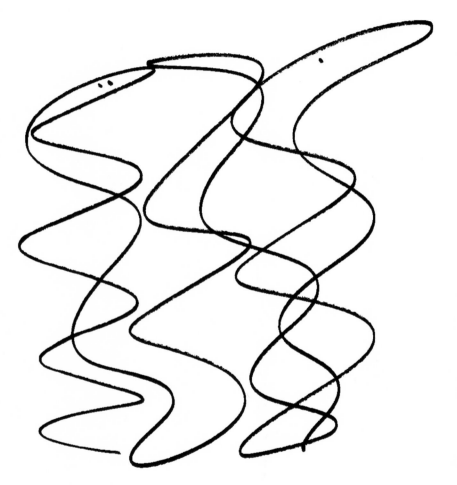

Look! If I told you once,
I told you a thousand times;
Once is never enough!

Who we are
Is often overshadowed
By who we think we are

Behind every great man
There's a secretary

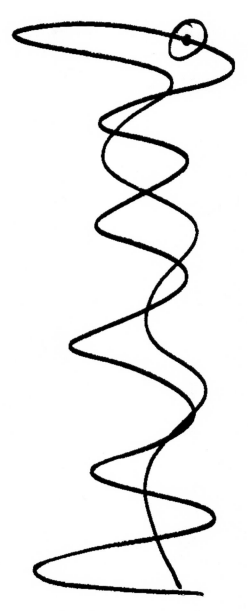

A friend in constant need
Needs help indeed

He, whose laugh lasts, laughs last.

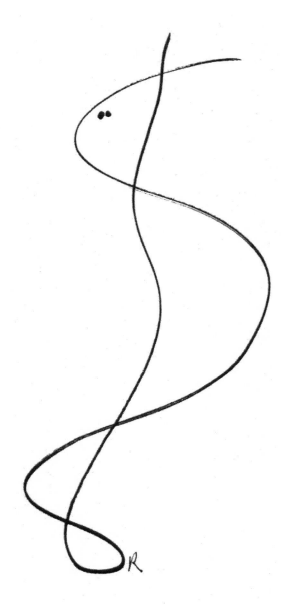

He who laughs last
Didn't get the joke
As fast as the others.

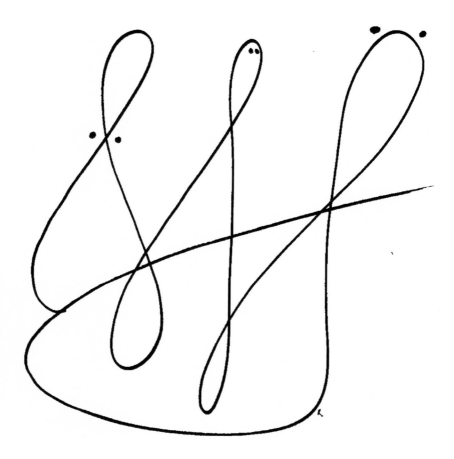

Which one doesn't belong?

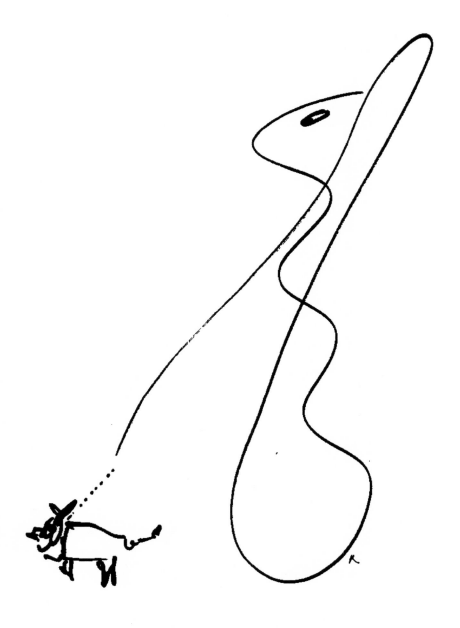

Dog walking squibble

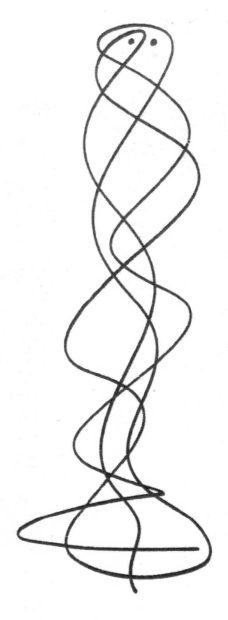

A squibble a day delays a visit to the doctor